Beetles

By Sandra Donovan

Steadwell Books

Raintree Steck-Vaughn Publishers

A Harcourt Company

Austin · New York

www.raintreesteckvaughn.com

ANIMALS OF THE RAIN FOREST

Published by Raintree Steck-Vaughn Publishers,
an imprint of Steck-Vaughn Company.

Library of Congress Cataloging-in-Publication Data
Printed and bound in the United States of America
1 2 3 4 5 6 7 8 9 10 WZ 05 04 03 02
ISBN 0-7398-5368-6

Produced by Compass Books

Photo Acknowledgments
Corbis/Papilio, 18, 22; Luiz Claudio Marigo, 6, 8, 11, 18, 24; Visuals Unlimited, cover;
Charles Phillip, 14; Ken Lucas, 16, 26; Jeff Daly, 21; Wildlife Conservation
Society/headquartered at the Bronx Zoo, D. DeMello, title page, 12, 28-29.

Editor: Bryon Cahill
Consultant: Sean Dolan

Content Consultant
Richard Mankin
United States Department of Agriculture

This book supports the National Science Standards.

Contents

MEXICO

BELIZE
HONDURAS
NICARAGUA
GUATEMALA
EL SALVADOR *Caribbean Sea*
COSTA RICA
PANAMA
ECUADOR

North Atlantic Ocean

GUYANA
SURINAME
VENEZUELA
FRENCH GUIANA (FRANCE)
COLOMBIA

PERU

AMAZON RIVER

BRAZIL

BOLIVIA

South Pacific Ocean

PARAGUAY

CHILE

South Atlantic Ocean

ARGENTINA   URUGUAY

Range of the Hercules Beetle

Surrounding Land

Water

Borders

Rivers

N
W · E
S

4

A Quick Look at Beetles

What do beetles look like?

Beetles come in many different sizes and colors. Some have horns on their heads. All beetles have wings, legs, eyes, and antennae.

Where do beetles live?

Beetles live almost everywhere in the world, except Antarctica. Many live in the rain forests of Africa, Australia, Central America, South America, and Southeast Asia.

What do beetles eat?

Different kinds of beetles eat different things. Many eat plants and fruits. Some eat insects, fish, or other animals. Other beetles eat food they find, such as animal droppings.

This harlequin beetle lives in the trees of the rain forest.

Beetles in the Rain Forest

There are more kinds of beetle than there are kinds of any other animal. All beetles are insects. An insect has six legs and a body that is divided into three parts. These three parts are the head, thorax (THO-raks), and **abdomen**. The abdomen holds the stomach. The thorax is between the head and the abdomen. Most insects also have wings.

The scientific name for beetles is *Coleoptera* (ko-lee-AHP-tuh-ruh). This word comes from two Greek words that mean "sheath wing." A sheath is a kind of cover. Beetles have two hard, front wings that cover their thin back wings like a sheath.

Beetles can live in a lot of different places. Many beetles live in rain forests. Rain forests are places where many trees and plants grow close together and much rain falls.

These helpful dung beetles are eating animal droppings.

Where Do Beetles Live?

Beetles live almost everywhere in the world, except very cold places like Antarctica. Many live in the rain forests of Africa, Australia, Central America, South America, and Southeast Asia.

Different kinds of beetle live in different habitats. A habitat is a place where an animal or plant usually lives. Rain forest beetles make their homes in many different areas of the forests. They can live in water, in trees, in plants, and on the ground.

Many beetles live in trees. They bore, or eat, their way into the inside of trees. This makes a round hole, like a tunnel. Beetles live inside these tunnels. Some kinds of beetle live under the bark on the outside of trees.

Ground beetles live on the floor of rain forests. At night, they often climb trees to look for food. In the morning, they come down and hide under plants or leaves on the ground.

Water beetles live in water. However, they still breathe air like other insects. Before swimming, they store air under their front wings. They breathe this air when they swim under water.

Beetles are an important part of the rain forest. Helpful beetles eat animal droppings and small insects. This keeps the forest cleaner. Helpful beetles also eat dying trees. The dying trees are then broken down and returned to the soil in beetle waste. This makes the soil richer so that new plants can grow. Harmful beetles kill plants, fruit, and trees. Some kinds of beetle can destroy fruit crops in the rain forest.

Kinds of Beetle

There are almost 300,000 different species of beetle in the world. A species is a group of animals or plants that share common features and are closely related to each other.

Beetle species are many sizes, too. They range from about 7 inches (18 cm) to smaller than the period at the end of this sentence. Most rain forest beetles are larger than beetles in other places. Scientists are not sure why this is true.

The world's largest beetle species is the giant hercules beetle. These beetles live in the rain forests of Central America. Hercules beetles are black and have two long horns on their head. They can grow to more than 7 inches (18 cm) long.

Longicornis beetles also live in the rain forests of Central America. These beetles live in the leaves of the rain forest trees. They are black and yellow and look like wasps.

The five-horned beetle lives in Southeast Asia. It has four short horns that point forward and one long horn that curves up from the top of its

This is a giant hercules beetle. It is the largest kind of beetle in the world.

head. Five-horned beetles are about
3 inches (8 cm) long.

African goliath beetles live in the rain forests of Africa. They are black with white lines and spots on them. Goliath beetles are about 4 inches (11 cm) long. They are the heaviest beetle in the world and weigh about 3.5 ounces (100 g).

All beetles have antennae, six legs, and three main body sections.

What Do Beetles Look Like?

Every species of beetle looks different. Still, they all have certain features in common. The beetle's mouth, eyes, and **antennae** are on its head. The antennae are two feelers that the beetle uses to touch and smell. Beetle antennae come in many different shapes and sizes. Some are thin feelers.

Some have clubs on their tips. Some are feathery, and others are like antlers.

The thorax is the middle part of the beetle. All beetles have three pairs of legs and two pairs of wings attached to the thorax.

The way they use their wings makes beetles different from other insects. The front wings fold down over the back wings. This hides and protects the back wings. When beetles fly, they first have to spread out their front wings. Then they can unfold the back wings. In flight, the front wings stay still, like the wings of an airplane, while the back wings move up and down.

Beetles can be many different colors. They may have stripes, spots, or other patterns on them. Some species are black or mostly black. Many beetles that live in rain forests are brightly colored. This camouflage helps them blend in with the trees and fruits around them. Camouflage is colors, shapes, and patterns that make something blend in with its background. For example, African tortoise beetles are yellow and green. This helps them blend in with the leaves they live on.

These two herbivore beetles are eating a peach.

What Beetles Eat

Beetles do not need to travel to find food. They usually eat the plants that they live on, or animals they live near. Beetles eat all kinds of plants and animals. Some water beetles eat fish. Others eat insects that fall into the water.

Beetles that eat only plant and tree parts are **herbivores**. Some herbivore beetles eat the soft part of trees found under the bark. Others drink the sap from trees. Beetles also eat flowers, leaves, stems, and roots of different rain forest plants.

Some beetles are also predators. Predators hunt other animals for food. Most beetle predators eat other insects. Some also eat snails, slugs, and worms.

Animals that look for food they did not kill are called scavengers. Scavenger beetles feed on dung or the bodies of dead insects or animals.

This water beetle is diving near underwater plants to catch an insect to eat.

Eating and Digesting Food

Beetles eat food with their mouth. When they eat, they do not chew their food very well. To help break down food, the stomach has a part called a **gizzard**. The gizzard crushes big pieces of food into tiny pieces.

The crushed food then travels through the rest of the beetle's stomach. There, water and nutrients are absorbed, or soaked, into the body. A nutrient is something that helps living things grow. Food the beetle cannot use is passed out of its body as waste.

Eating Habits

Different species of beetle have different eating habits. A habit is a usual way of doing something. Beetles that eat plants may eat many small meals each day. For example, beetles that live in trees may eat all day long as they chew their way along the inside of a tree.

Beetles that eat insects may eat only once every day or every other day. These beetles digest an insect very slowly so that the food lasts longer. Digest means to break down food so the body can use it.

Other beetles digest food quickly. They may need to eat many small insects each day. For example, a ladybug eats very small insects called aphids. One ladybug can eat as many as 60 aphids in one day.

Beetles use special scents to find each other during mating season.

A Beetle's Life Cycle

Most beetles mate only during their breeding season. In the rain forest, this season is often early spring. Males and females of the same species will mate if they meet during breeding season.

Beetles find mates in different ways. Some species of beetle may find mates when they are feeding. Other beetles use scents to find mates. These beetles release a scent that other beetles of the same species can smell from far away. A beetle will follow this scent until it finds a mate.

There are other ways beetles attract mates, too. Female fireflies glow at night so passing males can find them. Death watch beetles make a noise by tapping their heads on wood to attract mates.

Eggs and Larvae

All female beetles lay eggs after they mate. Some beetles, such as dung beetles, lay only one egg at a time. Other beetles lay up to 300 eggs at once. They lay their eggs in leaves, under ground, inside trees, or other places where they live.

The egg is the first of the four stages in a beetle's life. The other stages are the **larva**, the **pupa**, and the adult beetle. **Metamorphosis** is the process of changing from one stage to the next.

Beetle eggs hatch into larvae. Larvae do not have wings. They look like small worms. This stage lasts for a few weeks for some beetles. For others, it can last for two or three years.

During this stage, larvae eat a lot of food and grow larger. A beetle is covered by a hard covering called an exoskeleton. The exoskeleton does not grow with the larva. In order to grow, the larva must shed its exoskeleton in a process called molting.

To molt, a larva eats and grows inside its exoskeleton. The exoskeleton becomes harder and tighter as the larva gets larger. While this is

▲ This photo shows the egg, larva, and
adult stage of a beetle's life.

happening, a soft, new exoskeleton grows
underneath the old, hard exoskeleton. Finally,
the exoskeleton splits. The larva crawls out of
the old exoskeleton and begins to eat again. It
will molt again when its new exoskeleton
becomes too small.

This stag beetle is in the pupa stage. A hard shell protects it while it changes to an adult.

 Throughout history, different people have worshiped beetles. The ancient Egyptians considered the scarab beetle to be a symbol of life after death. This is why many Egyptian tombs, or graves, have drawings of scarab beetles on them. Also, a tribe in South America believed that a huge beetle was the creator of Earth. Some Europeans believed that killing the dor beetle would cause bad luck and storms.

Pupa and Adults

The larva changes to a pupa after its last larval molt. When it becomes a pupa, a hard shell grows over it. Inside the shell, the body changes from the larva to the adult beetle. It grows wings and legs. This usually takes about one month.

Finally, the hard shell splits open. The adult beetle crawls out. It has now entered its final life stage. As an adult, it finds a mate and produces young. Different species of beetle can live from a few days to several years.

This elephant beetle's brown color helps it blend in with the trees where it lives.

The Future of Beetles

Today, almost one in every four animals on Earth is a beetle. This makes beetles the most common animal on our planet.

Scientists think that beetles have been around for more than 230 million years. One way they know this is from finding very old beetle fossils. Fossils are outlines or remains left by animals that lived long ago.

Scientists think beetles have survived because they **adapt** well. To adapt means to change in order to fit your surroundings. Beetles have adapted in different ways. For example, they have found many unusual places to live and hide. Some beetles live or hide underground, or inside plants, trees, and seeds.

| This is a giant metallic ceiba wood-boring beetle. It hides in tunnels it makes in trees.

Surviving in the Rain Forest

All beetles have to avoid predators. Predators are animals that hunt other animals for food. Almost all animals are predators of beetles, including birds, fish, and other insects.

Beetles are built to protect themselves from their enemies. Their hard front wings fold down over most of their body. This helps protect them from some predators.

Beetles are very strong. A Betsy beetle can pull seven and a half times its own weight. A horse can pull only about half its own weight. This makes the beetle about 15 times stronger than a horse!

Beetles also have other ways of keeping safe. Some beetles make chemicals that smell bad or taste bad. They release these chemicals to warn enemies not to come near. Some species play dead. They fold their wings and drop to the ground when predators are near. Some predators may leave if they think the beetles are dead.

Some beetles survive because they are able to move very quickly. This helps them escape from their enemies. It also helps them move to new places to live when the weather changes. Beetles in the rain forest can quickly find dry areas during the rainy season.

Because beetles adapt so well, they are not in danger of becoming **extinct**. Extinct means that all of that kind of animal has died out. Scientists believe that beetles will be around for a long time.

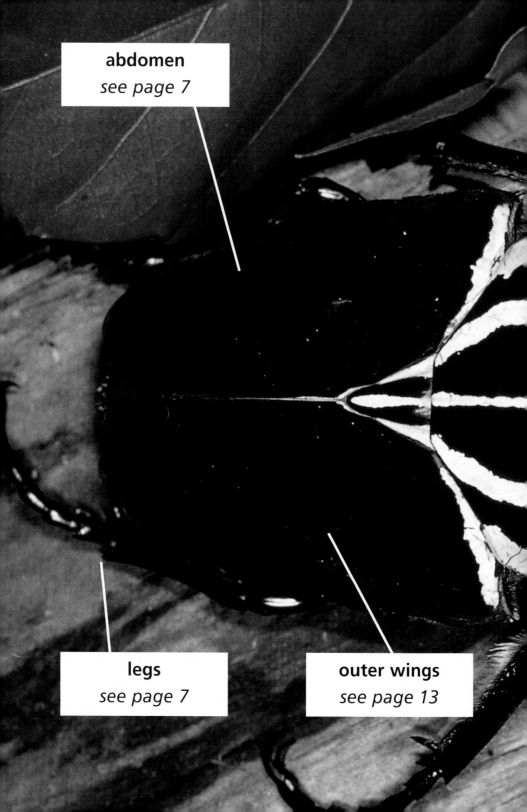

abdomen
see page 7

legs
see page 7

outer wings
see page 13

thorax
see page 7

head
see page 7

antennae
see page 12

Glossary

abdomen (AB-duh-men)—part of an insect's body that holds its stomach

adapt (a-DAHPT)—when a plant or animal changes to fit the area where it lives

antennae (an-TEN-ay)—two thin feelers on a beetle's head that it uses for touching and smelling

extinct (ek-STINKT)—when all of one kind of animal has died out

gizzard (GIH-zard)—part of a beetle's stomach where its food is crushed

herbivores (ER-bih-vors)—animals that eat only plants and tree parts

larva (LAR-vah)—the second stage in a beetle's life cycle

metamorphosis (met-uh-MOR-fuh-sis)—the process of changing from one stage to another

pupa (PEW-puh)—the third stage in a beetle's life cycle

Internet Sites

Rain Forest Action Network: Kid's Corner
www.ran.org/kids_action

Rain Forest Insects
rainforest-australia.com/insects1.htm

Useful Address

The Coleopterist's Society
23 D'Evereaux Street
Natchez, MS 39120

Books to Read

Hipp, Andrew. *Dung Beetles.* New York:
PowerKids Press, 2002.

Murray, Peter. *Beetles.* Chanhassen, MN: Child's
World, 2002.

Index